LITTLE LUCY'S GOOD LUCK
© 2020 by Galeron Consulting Group.

All rights reserved. Printed in the United States of America. No part of this book may be used or reproduced in any manner whatsoever without written permission except in the case of brief quotations embodied in critical articles or reviews.

This book is a work of fiction. Names, characters, businesses, organizations, places, events and incidents either are the product of the author's imagination or are used fictitiously. Any resemblance to actual persons, living or dead, events, or locales is entirely coincidental.

10 9 8 7 6 5 4 3 2 1
ISBN: 978-1-63514-855-8

For information visit:
GALERON CONSULTING GROUP
PUBLISHING DIVISION
website: www.galeronbooks.com

LITTLE LUCY
GOOD LUCK
COLORING BOOK

Little Lucy was very lucky, but she didn't know it. Lucy thought she was going to be really lucky after finding the four-leaf clover. But it didn't seem to work. When she saw the four-leaf clover, at first she was excited. She thought that having good luck meant winning the lottery or being picked to be a famous star. She didn't know that luck came in all shapes in sizes. If that four-leaf clover didn't bring her good luck that day, Lucy would have been in so much trouble! If only she knew how lucky she was that day!

This book belongs to:

_____